Beginners

Japanese

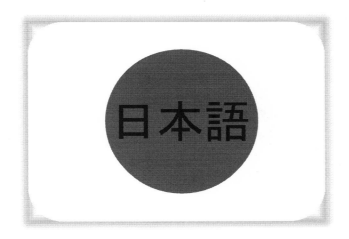

日本語

Kana - Hiragana
& Katakana

BEGINNERS JAPANESE

Hiragana & Katakana

HIRAGANA & KATAKANA

Start your journey into learning how to read and write Japanese by taking on both the first and the second alphabets. This workbook takes you through each character and modified character with hints and tips to help you build your knowledge as you go. Practice sheets are included in each section to allow you to practice each character, refine your writing skills and try some sample words.

Danny Asser

Study Hiragana Contents

Stage One & Introduction

See Hiragana in real life examples, as it is used in Japan today.

Basic Hiragana characters and associated sounds. Practice writing each character and then some sample words using the characters you have just learnt

Stage Two

Modified standard Hiragana characters. Learn which Hiragana can be modified to make alternative sounds by using small symbols that follow each standard character

Stage Three

Review the full suite of characters with the last set of modifiers. Small versions of the standard characters that provide even more alternative ways to pronounce words

Beginners Japanese – Hiragana Stage One

The Japanese Alphabet(s)

When starting out learning to read and write Japanese it is important to start with the building blocks of the language. Japanese uses three collections of characters to construct words and sentences.

The first is called **Hiragana** ひらがな

Hiragana is made up of characters that represent the vowels and other syllables. These are compiled to create the words, such as Hi(ひ) Ra(ら) Ga(が) Na(な) (Hiragana) foreign language students as well as Japanese children start by learning the characters of Hiragana. A basic form of pronunciation for most words is simply sticking to the sounds of the separate syllables, as with Hi-Ra-Ga-Na above.

You will notice that each column and each row have a title as these refer to the content of each syllable in the chart.

	A	I	U	E	O
Vowels	あ (A)	い (I)	う (U)	え (E)	お (O)
K	か (Ka)	き (Ki)	く (Ku)	け (Ke)	こ (Ko)
S	さ (Sa)	し (Shi)	す (Su)	せ (Se)	そ (So)
T	た (Ta)	ち (Chi)	つ (Tsu)	て (Te)	と (To)
N	な (Na)	に (Ni)	ぬ (Nu)	ね (Ne)	の (No)
H	は (Ha)	ひ (Hi)	ふ (Fu)	へ (He)	ほ (Ho)
M	ま (Ma)	み (Mi)	む (Mu)	め (Me)	も (Mo)
Y	や (Ya)		ゆ (Yu)		よ (Yo)
R	ら (Ra)	り (Ri)	る (Ru)	れ (Re)	ろ (Ro)
W	わ (Wa)				を (Wo)
N	ん (N)				

The rows K, S, T etc refer to the first letter of each syllable and the columns (A-I-U-E-O) to the second letter. There are of course some exceptions and these are highlighted.

Many of these characters can also be modified to create more sounds such as と (To) can be changed to ど (Do) there are other examples that we will come to later.

Some Hiragana characters also have special uses within sentences, such as の, は, つ, に, and を. It may seem complex now but will start to become clearer as your study of Japanese continues.

6

Translated public sign using Katakana, then Kanji and Hiragana, then two Kanji again

The other character sets used in the Japanese language are:

Katakana かたかな , or when written in Katakana カタカナ.

Katakana is mainly used to represent words that are of foreign origin to the Japanese and is made up of the same sounds shown for Hiragana above. This means that when common Western words are translated into Katakana, they can sound a little different. Typically, they resemble the English equivalent word but the sounds are formed using the sounds of each Katakana symbol. Although there are many symbols and therefore sounds in both Hiragana and Katakana some English ones are not available.

A Tokyo Rail Station sign using Kanji at the top, Hiragana at the centre and Roman characters at the bottom. This last translation at the bottom uses a line over the letter o to indicate an extended sound when pronounced. Written in full the word would be Toukyou

Kanji かんじ or 漢字. The second set of characters are both Kanji, Kanji were derived originally from the Chinese language and make up most of written Japanese when combined with some Hiragana and of course some words from Katakana.

One easy way to tell if a piece of writing is written in Chinese or in Japanese is to look for the Hiragana or Katakana within it. If the text is only comprised of Kanji then it is likely to be Chinese.

It is said that to be considered literate in Japan you should be able to read and understand 10,000 Kanji. With these 10,000 Kanji you should be able to read a common newspaper.

Real World Examples

You should be able to tell from the shapes on these buttons what they do when I tell you they are from a lift. As in the USA, Japanese usually refer to it as an elevator.

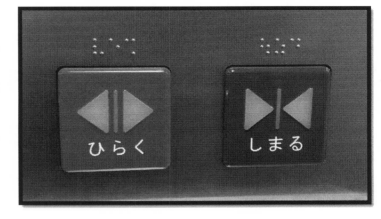

The green button is to open the doors, Hiraku (ひらく) and the black button to close the doors Shimaru (しまる).

You may also notice that, above the buttons, braille is used. This is very common in Japan, and is accompanied by pavement markers and pedestrian crossings with loud bird noises when they turn green (usually silent) at least around Tokyo and other large city areas.

The two signs above can be found on the steps in and out of a railway station in an attempt to get people to stick to just one side. This is not always easy as the correct side to be on does switch around from station to station, as it does in other countries too. Both words *Nobori* or up (のぼり) and *Kudari* or down (くだり) contain one modified character from Stage two of this book.

Writing your first Japanese Letters.

Let's get back to Hiragana and to practicing writing the letters that we will learn in order to write our first sentences in Japanese. Try to recreate each character in the boxes below. All Japanese characters will look slightly different in your own handwriting, get as close as you can to the printed versions.

Use the grey characters in the second column to help you practice the shape.

あ	あ							
い	い							
う	う							
え	え							
お	お							

K Hiragana Practice

か	か								
き	き								
く	く								
け	け								
こ	こ								

Sample Words Practice 1

If you have practiced the ten characters above you will already be able to write these words in Japanese:

Train Station (Eki) えき   Tree (Ki) き   No (iie) いいえ   Red (Aka)   あか

Big (Ooki) おおき

Practice these sample words below:

えき	えき			
き	き			
いいえ	いいえ			
あか	あか			
おおき	おおき			

Character Memory Test

Try to identify the Hiragana character in the centre, which letter or sound does it represent?
Check your answer at the table on the introduction page.

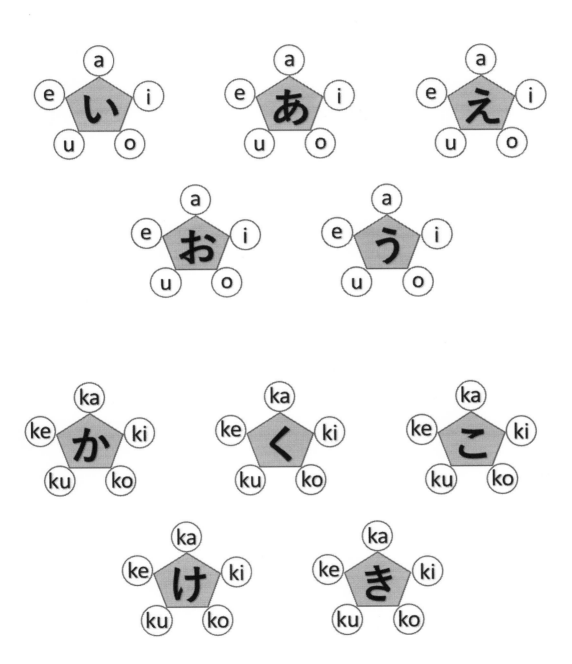

S Hiragana Practice

さ	さ							
し	し							
す	す							
せ	せ							
そ	そ							

A common exception to the pronunciation rule is the symbol Su (す). When Su is used as part of a word, only the S is pronounced. SuKi or すき is translated as *to like* and DeSu or です as *it is*. Commonly these two words are used together in a sentence as SuKi DeSu or すきです meaning "I like it". Both uses of Su here are pronounced just as S so the pronunciation becomes Ski—Des.

T Hiragana Practice

た	た									
ち	ち									
つ	つ									
て	て									
と	と									

Sample Words Practice 2

If you have practiced the ten characters above you will already be able to write these words in Japanese:

Small (Chiisai) ちいさい   Nice (Suteki) すてき   Good (ii) いい   When? (itsu) いつ
Underground/Subway (Chikatetsu) ちかてつ Practice these sample words below:

ちいさい	ちいさい			
すてき	すてき			
いい	いい			
いつ	いつ			
ちかてつ	ちかてつ			

Note on pronunciation. When saying Suteki the u sound is dropped from Su (as mentioned earlier) to make the word sound more like *Stekki*. Additionally the character Tsu つ is pronounced as in the common word Tsunami, otherwise known as a tidal wave.

Character Memory Test

Try to identify the Hiragana character in the centre, which letter or sound does it represent?
Check your answer at the table on the introduction page.

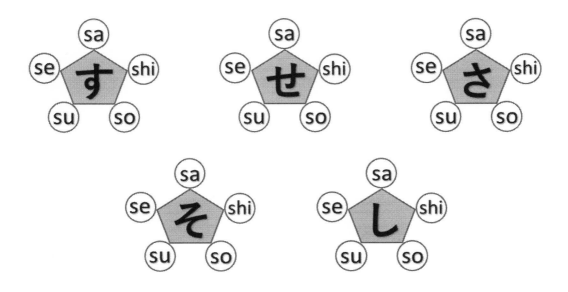

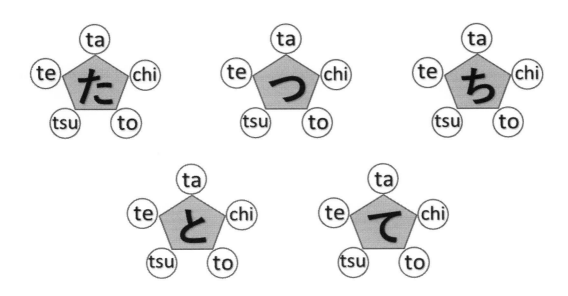

N Hiragana Practice

な	な								
に	に								
ぬ	ぬ								
ね	ね								
の	の								

H Hiragana Practice

は	は									
ひ	ひ									
ふ	ふ									
へ	へ									
ほ	ほ									

Sample Words Practice 3

If you have practiced the ten characters from N and H groups above you will already be able to write these words in Japanese:

What (Nani) なに　　Chopsticks (Hashi)はし　　Flower (Hana) はな　　Want (Hoshii)ほしい
Money (Okane)　おかね

Practice these sample words below:

なに	なに			
はし	はし			
はな	はな			
ほしい	ほしい			
おかね	おかね			

Character Memory Test

Try to identify the Hiragana character in the centre, which letter or sound does it represent?
Check your answer at the table on the introduction page.

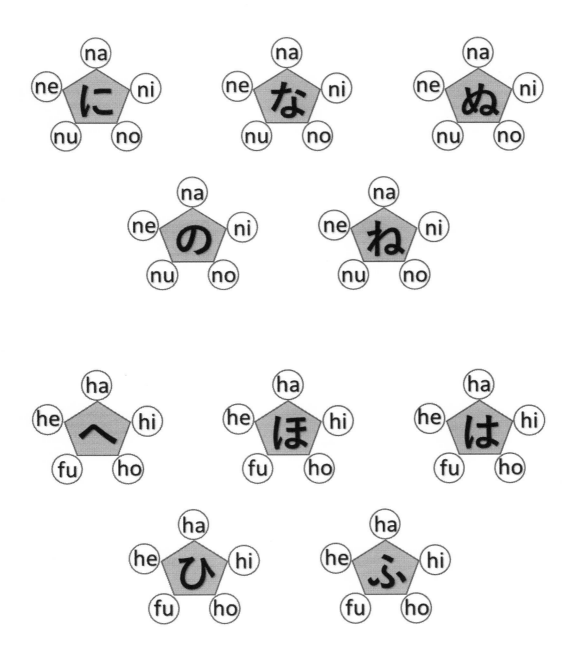

M Hiragana Practice

ま	ま								
み	み								
む	む								
め	め								
も	も								

Y Hiragana Practice

や	や									
ゆ	ゆ									
よ	よ									

Character Memory Test

Try to identify the Hiragana character in the centre, which letter or sound does it represent?
Check your answer at the table on the introduction page.

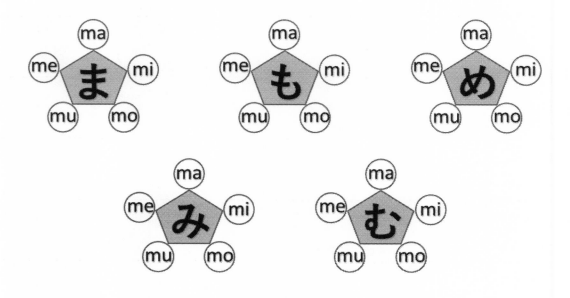

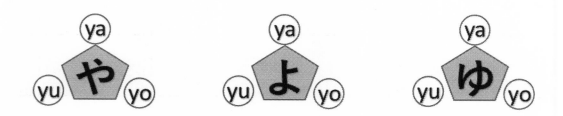

R Hiragana Practice

ら	ら								
り	り								
る	る								
れ	れ								
ろ	ろ								

While Ru る and Ro ろ are very similar you will notice the loop at the bottom of the Ru る character.

W and small n Hiragana Practice

わ	わ							
を	を							
ん	ん							

Although often read as just O, を is often spelt in English (sometimes referred to as roman) characters as Wo. The term used for English characters when used to spell Japanese words is Romaji.

Character Memory Test

Try to identify the Hiragana character in the centre, which letter or sound does it represent?
Check your answer at the table on the introduction page.

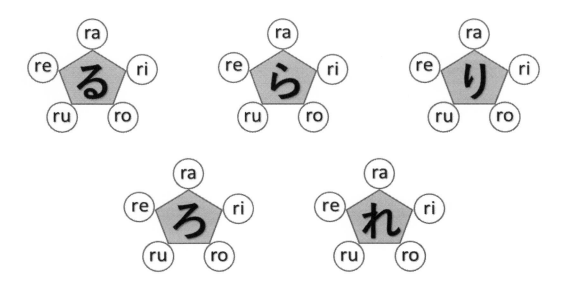

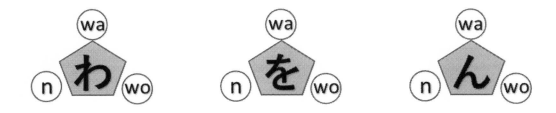

Sample Words Practice 4

If you have practiced all of the Hiragana groups above you will already be able to write these words in Japanese:

Teacher (Sensei) せんせい   Goodbye (Sayonara) さよなら   Excuse Me (Sumimasen) すみません
Book (Hon) ほん   Japan (Nihon) にほん

Practice these sample words below:

せんせい	せんせい		
さよなら	さよなら		
すみません	すみません		
ほん	ほん		
にほん	にほん		

Fill in the blank characters Test

Use your memory of the characters and your new handwriting skills to fill in the missing Hiragana below.

	A	I	U	E	O
Vowels	あ (A)	__(I)	う (U)	__(E)	お (O)
K	__(Ka)	き (Ki)	__(Ku)	け (Ke)	__(Ko)
S	さ (Sa)	__(Shi)	__(Su)	__(Se)	そ (So)
T	__(Ta)	__(Chi)	つ (Tsu)	__(Te)	__(To)
N	な (Na)	__(Ni)	__(Nu)	__(Ne)	の (No)
H	__(Ha)	ひ (Hi)	__(Fu)	へ (He)	__(Ho)
M	ま (Ma)	__(Mi)	む (Mu)	__(Me)	も (Mo)
Y	や (Ya)		__(Yu)		よ (Yo)
R	__(Ra)	り (Ri)	__(Ru)	れ (Re)	__(Ro)
W	わ (Wa)				__(Wo)
N	__(N)				

Beginners Japanese – Hiragana Stage Two

Modified basic Hiragana Characters

	A	I	U	E	O
Vowels	あ (A)	い (I)	う (U)	え (E)	お (O)
K	か (Ka)	き (Ki)	く (Ku)	け (Ke)	こ (Ko)
S	さ (Sa)	し (Shi)	す (Su)	せ (Se)	そ (So)
T	た (Ta)	ち (Chi)	つ (Tsu)	て (Te)	と (To)
N	な (Na)	に (Ni)	ぬ (Nu)	ね (Ne)	の (No)
H	は (Ha)	ひ (Hi)	ふ (Fu)	へ (He)	ほ (Ho)
M	ま (Ma)	み (Mi)	む (Mu)	め (Me)	も (Mo)
Y	や (Ya)		ゆ (Yu)		よ (Yo)
R	ら (Ra)	り (Ri)	る (Ru)	れ (Re)	ろ (Ro)
W	わ (Wa)				を (Wo)
N	ん (N)				

The second group of Hiragana characters are essentially modified versions of the first chart, shown here on the left.

Not every character from the first chart is modified. The full list is shown below.

The modifications change the sound of the character and are indicated above and to the right of the character as it is written.

You will notice the Ga が from Hiragana appears below from the modified Ka か character.

G	が (Ga)	ぎ (Gi)	ぐ (Gu)	げ (Ge)	ご (Go)
Z	ざ (Za)	じ (Ji)	ず (Zu)	ぜ (Ze)	ぞ (Zo)
D	だ (Da)			で (De)	ど (Do)
B	ば (Ba)	び (Bi)	ぶ (Bu)	べ (Be)	ぼ (Bo)
P	ぱ (Pa)	ぴ (Pi)	ぷ (Pu)	ぺ (Pe)	ぽ (Po)

You will notice that 〝 modifies the sound from Ka to Ga or from Te to De etc.

º Generally modifies a character to a P sound for example Ha becomes Pa, as shown below.

Ka (か) Ga (が)

Ha (は) Ba (ば) Pa (ぱ)

Hi (ひ) Bi (び) Pi (ぴ)

Te (て) De (で)

Real World Examples

Silver Dara fish shown here above provide an example of the way Japanese is presented to the viewer in Japan. The first character is a Kanji meaning silver(銀) with the two Hiragana characters that follow spelling Dara (だら).

Once again to the left, another fish (ぶり) or pronounced *Buri* – Japanese Amberjack. The Kanji for Yen the Japanese currency is also shown below the name in both examples (円).

In this example we can see some dried Sardines (めざし) or *Mezashi*. You will note the handwritten style at the top left of the picture does look different to that of the printed labels on the packets of fish.

Also, with this example you can see the use of the international symbol for Yen (¥) rather than the kanji shown in the example above. They are both used widely in Japan.

Here Yakisoba noodles are sold for ¥300 in a bun. You can see that Yakisoba, being a Japanese word is written in Hiragana (やきそば). You can also see the difference in writing, even between printed fonts, that provides a challenge when trying to read Hiragana.

Writing Japanese Letters – G Hiragana Practice.

Let's get back to practicing writing the letters that we will learn in order to write our first sentences in Japanese. Try to recreate each character in the boxes below. All Japanese characters will look slightly different in your own handwriting, get as close as you can to the printed versions.

While this may feel a little repetitive it will make your handwriting in Hiragana start to take shape and help you remember the characters with repeated practice.

が	が								
ぎ	ぎ								
ぐ	ぐ								
げ	げ								
ご	ご								

Z Hiragana Practice

ざ	ざ									
じ	じ									
ず	ず									
ぜ	ぜ									
ぞ	ぞ									

Sample Words Practice 1

If you have practiced the modified characters above, along with the previous lessons basic Hiragana characters, you will be able to write these words in Japanese:

English language (Eigo) えいご   Japanese Language (Nihongo 日本語) にほんご
Student (Gakusei) がくせい   Japanese Complex Writing Characters (Kanji) かんじ
Film (Eiga) えいが

Practice these sample words below:

えいご	えいご		
にほんご	にほんご		
がくせい	がくせい		
かんじ	かんじ		
えいが	えいが		

Character Memory Test

Try to identify the Hiragana character in the centre, which letter or sound does it represent?
Check your answer at the table on the introduction page.

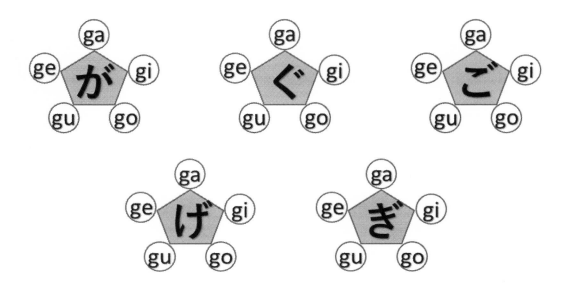

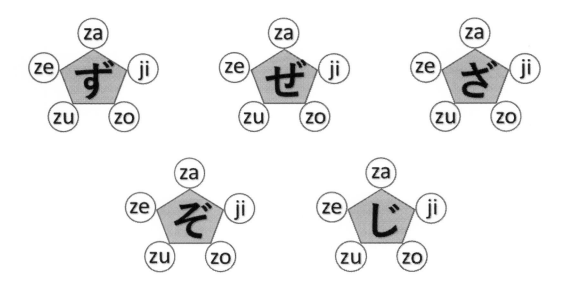

D Hiragana Practice

だ	だ								
で	で								
ど	ど								

B Hiragana Practice

ば	ば								
び	び								
ぶ	ぶ								
べ	べ								
ぼ	ぼ								

Sample Words Practice 2

If you have practiced the characters above you will already be able to write these words in Japanese:

Newspaper (Shinbun) しんぶん　　Thanks (Arigatou)　ありがとう　　Who (Dare) だれ
University (Daigaku)だいがく　　　　Where (Doko)　どこ

Practice these sample words below:

しんぶん	しんぶん		
ありがとう	ありがとう		
だれ	だれ		
だいがく	だいがく		
どこ	どこ		

Note on pronunciation. When saying Dare the two syllables are pronounced one at a time as in Da then Re, Da-Re, and not as in English for the word Dare.

P Hiragana Practice

ぱ	ぱ									
ぴ	ぴ										
ぷ	ぷ										
ぺ	ぺ										
ぽ	ぽ										

Sample Words Practice 3

If you have practiced the characters from the P group above you will already be able to write these words in Japanese, the P group characters are used less often in Hiragana than the other characters:

Pencil (Enpitsu) えんぴつ   Worry (Shinpai) しんぱい   A Toast (Kanpai) かんぱい

Walk (Sanpo) さんぽ   Tempura-*Japanese cooking style* てんぷら

Practice these sample words below:

えんぴつ	えんぴつ		
しんぱい	しんぱい		
かんぱい	かんぱい		
さんぽ	さんぽ		
てんぷら	てんぷら		

Sample Words Practice 4

If you have practiced all of the modified Hiragana groups above you will already be able to write these words in Japanese:

What time (Nanji) なんじ   Number (Bangou)ばんごう   A Person (Hito) ひと
Egg (Tomago)とまご   Fruit (Kudamono) くだもの

Practice these sample words below:

なんじ	なんじ		
ばんごう	ばんごう		
ひと	ひと		
とまご	とまご		
くだもの	くだもの		

Character Memory Test

Try to identify the Hiragana character in the centre, which letter or sound does it represent?
Check your answer at the table on the introduction page.

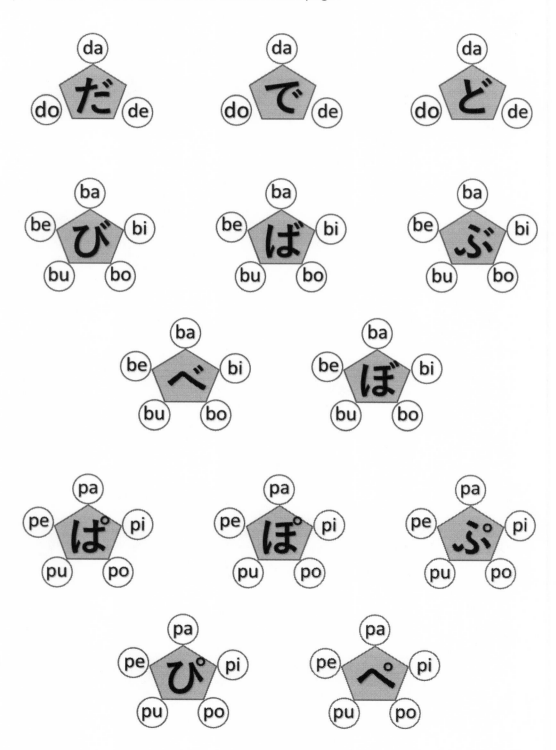

Fill in the blank characters Test

Use your memory of the characters and your new handwriting skills to fill in the missing Hiragana below.

G	が (Ga)	__(Gi)	ぐ(Gu)	__(Ge)	ご(Go)
Z	__(Za)	じ (Ji)	__(Zu)	__(Ze)	ぞ(Zo)
D	__(Da)			__(De)	ど(Do)
B	ば (Ba)	__(Bi)	__(Bu)	べ (Be)	__(Bo)
P	__(Pa)	ぴ (Pi)	ぷ (Pu)	__(Pe)	__(Po)

Beginners Japanese – Hiragana Stage Three

Modified Small Hiragana Characters

The Hiragana characters we have covered previously are shown below, new columns have been added to show the modifying characters. You will recognise them as a smaller version of the characters Ya, Yu and Yo from the Y row of Hiragana characters:

	A	I	U	E	O	Ya	Yu	Yo
Vowels	あ (A)	い (I)	う (U)	え (E)	お (O)			
K	か (Ka)	き(Ki)	く (Ku)	け (Ke)	こ (Ko)	きゃ(Kya)	きゅ(Kyu)	きょ(Kyo)
S	さ(Sa)	し (Shi)	す (Su)	せ (Se)	そ(So)	しゃ(Sha)	しゅ(Shu)	しょ(Sho)
T	た (Ta)	ち (Chi)	つ (Tsu)	て(Te)	と(To)	ちゃ(Cha)	ちゅ(Chu)	ちょ(Cho)
N	な (Na)	に(Ni)	ぬ (Nu)	ね (Ne)	の (No)	にゃ(Nya)	にゅ(Nyu)	にょ(Nyo)
H	は (Ha)	ひ (Hi)	ふ (Fu)	へ (He)	ほ (Ho)	ひゃ(Hya)	ひゅ(Hyu)	ひょ(Hyo)
M	ま(Ma)	み (Mi)	む (Mu)	め (Me)	も(Mo)	みゃ(Mya)	みゅ(Myu)	みよ(Myo)
Y	や (Ya)		ゆ (Yu)		よ(Yo)			
R	ら(Ra)	り (Ri)	る (Ru)	れ (Re)	ろ(Ro)	りゃ(Rya)	りゅ(Ryu)	りょ(Ryo)
W	わ (Wa)				を (Wo)			
N	ん (N)							

You will notice that each column and each row have a title as these refer to the content of each syllable in the chart.

The second group of Hiragana characters are essentially modified versions of the first chart. Not every character from the first chart is modified. The full list is shown below with the additional modifiers shown again in new columns.

G	が (Ga)	ぎ(Gi)	ぐ(Gu)	げ(Ge)	ご (Go)	ぎゃ(Gya)	ぎゅ(Gyu)	ぎょ(Gyo)
Z	ざ(Za)	じ (Ji)	ず (Zu)	ぜ (Ze)	ぞ(Zo)	じゃ(Ja)	じゅ(Ju)	じょ(Jo)
D	だ(Da)			で(De)	ど(Do)			
B	ば (Ba)	び(Bi)	ぶ (Bu)	べ (Be)	ぼ (Bo)	びゃ(Bya)	びゅ(Byu)	びょ(Byo)
P	ぱ (Pa)	ぴ (Pi)	ぷ (Pu)	ぺ (Pe)	ぽ (Po)	ぴゃ(Pya)	ぴゅ(Pyu)	ぴょ(Pyo)

As before you will notice that **"** modifies the sound from Ka to Ga or from Te to De etc.

º Generally modifies a character to a P sound for example Ha becomes Pa, as shown below.

つ A smaller version of Tsu is used to double the sound of the character that follows it and is seen often in Hiragana. Placed before Ka for example it becomes Kka when pronounced.

Writing Japanese Letters – Modified K Hiragana Practice.

Let's get back to practicing writing the letters that we will learn in order to write our first sentences in Japanese. Try to recreate each character in the boxes below. All Japanese characters will look slightly different in your own handwriting, get as close as you can to the printed versions.

While this may feel a little repetitive it will make your handwriting in Hiragana start to take shape and help you remember the characters with repeated practice.

Remember that the modifiers are just smaller versions of Ya, Yu and Yo that you learned in lesson 1 and these are always used after the character that they modify.

きゃ	きゃ						
きゅ	きゅ						
きょ	きょ						

Modified S Hiragana Practice

しゃ	しゃ						
しゅ	しゅ						
しょ	しょ						

Modified T Hiragana Practice

Although in the T group Chi is an exception as it begins with C of course. As with the others groups only one character is modified with Ya, Yu and Yo, in this case Chi ち is modified.

ちゃ	ちゃ						
ちゅ	ちゅ						
ちょ	ちょ						

Modified N Hiragana Practice

This time only the character Ni に is modified with Ya, Yu and Yo.

にゃ	にゃ						
にゅ	にゅ						
によ	によ						

Character Memory Test

Try to identify the Hiragana character in the centre, which letter or sound does it represent?
Check your answer at the table on the introduction page.

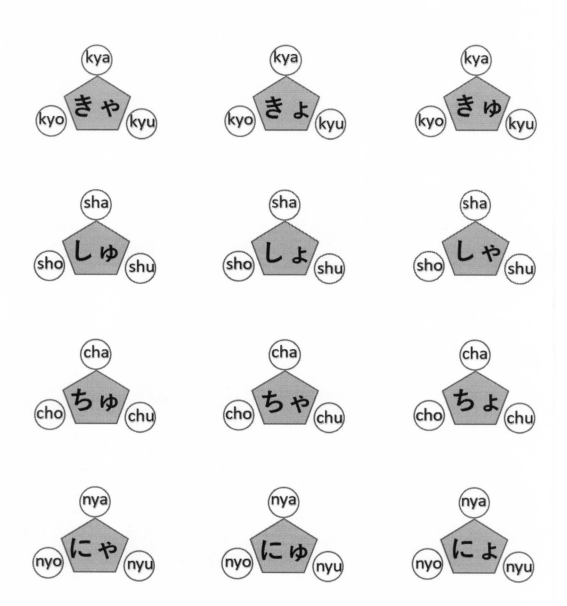

Modified H Hiragana Practice

ひゃ	ひゃ						
ひゅ	ひゅ						
ひょ	ひょ						

Modified M Hiragana Practice

みゃ	みゃ						
みゅ	みゅ						
みょ	みょ						

Modified R Hiragana Practice

りゃ	りゃ						
りゅ	りゅ						
りょ	りょ						

Modified G Hiragana Practice

ぎゃ	ぎゃ						
ぎゅ	ぎゅ						
ぎょ	ぎょ						

Character Memory Test

Try to identify the Hiragana character in the centre, which letter or sound does it represent?
Check your answer at the table on the introduction page.

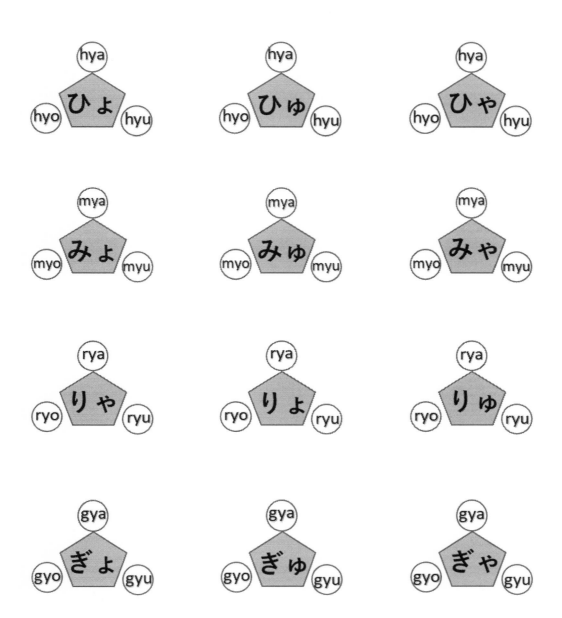

Modified Z Hiragana Practice

Again, the Z character modified here is an exception in that it starts with Ji and not Z like Za, Zu Ze and Zo.

じゃ	じゃ						
じゅ	じゅ						
じょ	じょ						

Modified B Hiragana Practice

びゃ	びゃ						
びゅ	びゅ						
びょ	びょ						

Modified P Hiragana Practice

ぴゃ	ぴゃ						
ぴゅ	ぴゅ						
ぴょ	ぴょ						

Character Memory Test

Try to identify the Hiragana character in the centre, which letter or sound does it represent?
Check your answer at the table on the introduction page.

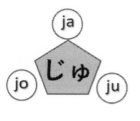 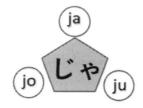 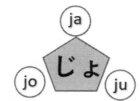

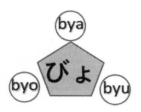 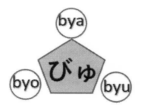 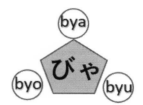

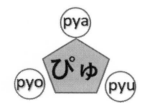 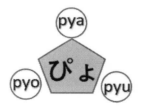 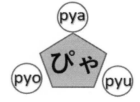

Writing Japanese Letters – Small Tsu つ Meaning.

When the Hiragana Tsu is used in the small form, such as in みっか meaning 3rd day of the month it doubles the hiragana sound that follows it. Please note that it no longer has any use as Tsu when presented as the small form of Tsu, it only indicates that the sound of the character that follows it in a word is doubled. This is shown as such: Mika (みか) or Mikka (みっか). Further examples of real words are shown below.

みっか 3rd day of month   よっつ four things or items   よっか 4th day of month

みっか	みっか				
よっつ	よっつ				
よっか	よっか				

Sample Words Practice 1

If you have practiced the Ya (や), Yu (ゆ) and Yo (よ) characters you can write these words in Japanese:

Homework (Shukudai) しゅくだい　 Tokyo (Japans Capital City) (Toukyou) とうきょう　　　 Travel or Trip (Ryokou) りょきょう　 Study (Benkyou) べんきょう　　 Weekend (Shuumatsu)　しゅうまつ

Practice these sample words below, remember that the や ゆ よ should be written noticeably smaller than the other characters when using to modify their sound:

しゅくだい	しゅくだい		
とうきょう	とうきょう		
りょきょう	りょきょう		
べんきょう	べんきょう		
しゅうまつ	しゅうまつ		

Sample Words Practice 2

Office (Jimusho) じむしょ   Hundred (Hyaku)ひゃく   Company (your office) (Kaisha) かいしゃ
Green Tea (Ocha) おちゃ   Photograph (Shashin)しゃしん

Practice these sample words below:

じむしょ	じむしょ			
ひゃく	ひゃく			
かいしゃ	かいしゃ			
おちゃ	おちゃ			
しゃしん	しゃしん			

Sample Words Practice 3

Milk (cows) (gyuunyuu) ぎゅうにゅう   Week (shuu) しゅう   Today (Kyou) きょう
Hospital (Byouin) びょういん   Dictionary (Jisho) じしょ

Practice these sample words below:

ぎゅうにゅう	ぎゅうにゅう		
しゅう	しゅう		
きょう	きょう		
びょういん	びょういん		
じしょ	じしょ		

Fill in the blank characters Test

Use your memory of the characters and your new handwriting skills to fill in the missing Hiragana below.

	A	I	U	E	O	Ya	Yu	Yo
Vowels	あ (A)	__(I)	う(U)	__(E)	お (O)			
K	__(Ka)	き (Ki)	__(Ku)	__(Ke)	こ(Ko)	__(Kya)	き ゆ(Kyu)	__(Kyo)
S	さ (Sa)	__(Shi)	す (Su)	__(Se)	そ(So)	しゃ(Sha)	__(Shu)	しょ(Sho)
T	__(Ta)	ち (Chi)	__(Tsu)	て (Te)	__(To)	ちゃ(Cha)	__(Chu)	ちょ(Cho)
N	__(Na)	__(Ni)	__(Nu)	__(Ne)	の (No)	にゃ(Nya)	__(Nyu)	にょ(Nyo)
H	__(Ha)	__(Hi)	ふ (Fu)	__(He)	ほ (Ho)	__(Hya)	__(Hyu)	ひょ(Hyo)
M	ま(Ma)	__(Mi)	__(Mu)	__(Me)	も(Mo)	__(Mya)	みゆ(Myu)	__(Myo)
Y	や (Ya)		__(Yu)		よ(Yo)			
R	__(Ra)	り (Ri)	__(Ru)	れ (Re)	__(Ro)	__(Rya)	りゆ(Ryu)	__(Ryo)
W	わ (Wa)				__(Wo)			
N	__(N)							

G	__(Ga)	__(Gi)	ぐ(Gu)	げ(Ge)	ご(Go)	__(Gya)	__(Gyu)	ぎょ(Gyo)
Z	__(Za)	__(Ji)	__(Zu)	ぜ (Ze)	ぞ(Zo)	じゃ(Ja)	__(Ju)	じょ(Jo)
D	だ (Da)			__(De)	__(Do)			
B	__(Ba)	__(Bi)	__(Bu)	べ (Be)	ぼ (Bo)	びゃ(Bya)	__(Byu)	__(Byo)
P	__(Pa)	__(Pi)	ぷ (Pu)	__(Pe)	__(Po)	__(Pya)	__(Pyu)	ぴょ(Pyo)

Essential Japanese From Hiragana

Numbers

	Simple Counting	One Thing (Shopping)	Date of the Month
One	いち	ひとつ	ついたち
Two	に	ふたつ	ふつか
Three	さん	みっつ	みっか
Four	し or よん	よっつ	よっか
Five	ご	いつつ	いつか
Six	ろく	むっつ	むいか
Seven	しち or なな	ななつ	なのか
Eight	はち	やっつ	ようか
Nine	く or きゅう	ここのつ	ここのか
Ten	じゅう	とお	とおか

Please note the difference between the small つ and the regular sized Tsu つ character in the tables.

People and Things Counting

	People	Age	Article of Clothing
One	ひとり	いっさい	いっちゃく
Two	ふたり	にさい	にちゃく
Three	さんにん	さんさい	さんちゃく
Four	よにん	よんさい	よんちゃく
Five	ごにん	ごさい	ごちゃく

Note the varied usage of the modifying small characters in both the charts above, small tsu is used to lengthen the sound of the character that follows and small ya (also small yo and yu) changes the character in front of it. Please refer back to the earlier sections of the workbook to refresh your memory if required.

Additional practice pages are provided next to allow further handwriting study, try writing some of the words above.

ひとつ	ひとつ			

ふたり	ふたり			
	ふたり			

BEGINNERS JAPANESE

Hiragana & Katakana

KATAKANA

Start your journey into learning how to read and write Japanese by taking on both the first and the second alphabets. This workbook takes you through each character and modified character with hints and tips to help you build your knowledge as you go.

Practice sheets are included in each section to allow you to practice each character, refine your writing skills and try some sample words.

Danny Asser

Study Katakana Contents

Stage One

The basic Katakana characters and associated sounds. Practice writing each character and then some sample words using the characters you have just learnt

Stage Two

Modified standard Katakana characters. Learn which Katakana can be modified to make alternative sounds by using small symbols that follow each standard character

Stage Three

Review the full suite of characters with the last set of modifiers. Small versions of the standard characters that provide even more alternative ways to pronounce words

Beginners Japanese – Katakana Stage One

The Japanese Alphabet(s)

When starting out learning to read and write Japanese it is important to start with the building blocks of the language. Japanese uses three collections of characters to construct words and sentences.

The second is called **Katakana** カタカナ

Katakana is made up of characters that represent the vowels and other syllables used in foreign words. These are compiled to create the words, such as Ka(カ) Ta(タ) Ka(か) Na(ナ) (Katakana) foreign language students as well as Japanese children start by learning the characters of Hiragana and Katakana. A basic form of pronunciation for most words can be simply sticking to the sounds of the separate syllables, as with Ka-Ta-Ka-Na above. When attempting pronunciation do not be tempted to use the English version of the word, that will sound very different to a Japanese person, they may not understand your version.

You will notice that each column and each row have a title as these refer to the content of each syllable in the chart.

	A	I	U	E	O
Vowels	ア (A)	イ (I)	ウ (U)	エ (E)	オ (O)
K	カ (Ka)	キ (Ki)	ク (Ku)	ケ (Ke)	コ (Ko)
S	サ (Sa)	シ (Shi)	ス (Su)	セ (Se)	ソ (So)
T	タ (Ta)	チ (Chi)	ツ (Tsu)	テ (Te)	ト (To)
N	ナ (Na)	ニ (Ni)	ヌ (Nu)	ネ (Ne)	ノ (No)
H	ハ (Ha)	ヒ (Hi)	フ (Fu)	ヘ (He)	ホ (Ho)
M	マ (Ma)	ミ (Mi)	ム (Mu)	メ (Me)	モ (Mo)
Y	ヤ (Ya)		ユ (Yu)		ヨ (Yo)
R	ラ (Ra)	リ (Ri)	ル (Ru)	れ (Re)	ロ (Ro)
W	ワ (Wa)				ヲ (Wo)
N	ン (N)				

The rows K, S, T etc refer to the first letter of each syllable and the columns (A-I-U-E-O) to the second letter. There are of course some exceptions and these are highlighted.

As with Hiragana, many of these characters can also be modified to create more sounds such as ト (To) can be changed to ド (Do) there are other examples that we will come to later.

The example here, Ringo is actually a shop name. It also happens to be the word for apple and its corresponding Katakana characters are spelt out below it. You will notice that the Go (ゴ) in RinGo is a modified Ko (コ)character.

It is common to mistake the characters Shi シ and Tsu ツ when used in Katakana. Shi is written using an upward stroke for the main shape of the character that may resemble a tick, and Tsu written with a downward stroke.

Similarities also exist with the characters for So ソ and No ノ both characters are written using a single downward stroke. With some fonts, such as the one used here, the only discernable difference is the small upward stroke to the left of the So ソ character. Again the character n ン is similar but with an upward long stroke and an upward short stroke.

An example of Katakana labelling taken from a sugar sachet.

Although it is becoming increasingly common to see English written on simple packaging and signage alongside the Katakana it becomes more rare outside major cities.

You can see signs like these commonly now in modern Tokyo and a few large cities. Some like this also borrow the symbols used when writing in English such as the & and ? symbols. These are not used in Japanese generally. Do not expect to see them commonly used outside of Tokyo just yet though.

In both of the examples here you will also notice short horizontal lines that indicate a lengthening of the character before it. Ta (タ) becomes Taa (ター) when pronounced, and so on.

You will notice that some of the labels on the right contain some Kanji characters. The top two spell out the English words below in the Japanese manner.

Although the bottom three examples to the right contain Kanji characters you will also notice that the last characters are in fact the same letters in Katakana. To i Re (トイレ) or Toilet.

Katakana is mainly used to represent words that are of foreign origin to the Japanese and is made up of the same sounds shown for Hiragana. This means that when common Western words are translated into Katakana, they can sound a little different. Typically, they resemble the English equivalent word but the sounds are formed using the sounds of each Katakana symbol. Although there are many symbols and therefore sounds in both Hiragana and Katakana some English ones are not available.

As in the example of toilet above, when talking to a Japanese speaker the pronunciation Toire (or phonetically *toy-ray*) will be understood more easily than saying Toilet.

Toire wa doko desu ka (where is the toilet?)

Toyray wa doko des ka

<u>トイレ</u>はどこですか

Only the underlined section of text is actually Katakana, the remainder is Hiragana.

Erebe-ta- wa doko desu ka (where is the elevator?)

Eribaytaa wa doko des ka

<u>エレベーター</u>はどこで
すか

The same question for finding the lift (elevator). Very useful in Tokyo and main city subways when carrying your luggage.

Writing your first Katakana Letters.

Let's get back to Katakana to practicing writing the letters that we will learn in order to write our first sentences in Japanese. Try to recreate each character in the boxes below. All Japanese characters will look slightly different in your own handwriting, get as close as you can to the printed versions.

ア	ア									
イ	イ									
ウ	ウ									
エ	エ									
オ	オ									

K Katakana Practice

カ	カ								
キ	キ								
ク	ク								
ケ	ケ								
コ	コ								

Character Memory Test

Try to identify the Hiragana character in the centre, which letter or sound does it represent?
Check your answer at the table on the introduction page.

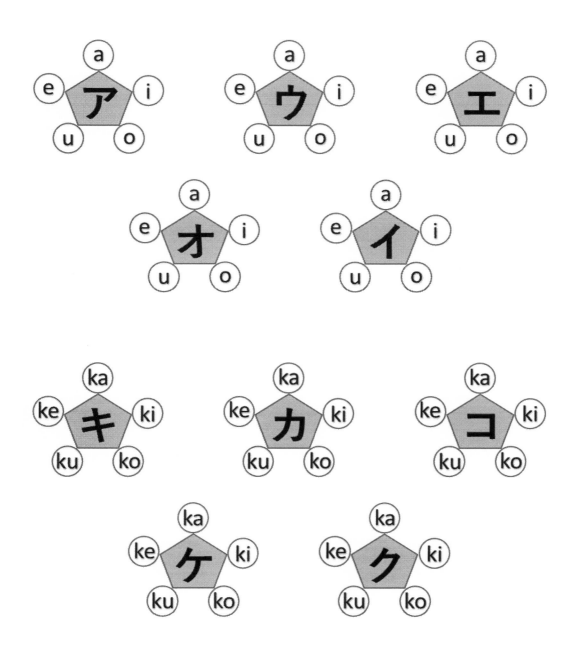

Sample Words Practice 1

Try writing these words in Katakana:

Australia (Oosutoraria) オーストラリア   America (Amerika) アメリカ   Tennis (Tenisu) テニス
Toilet (Toire) トイレ   Tomato (Tomato) トマト

Practice these sample words below:

オースラリア	オースラリア		
アメリカ	アメリカ		
テニス	テニス		
トイレ	トイレ		
トマト	トマト		

S Katakana Practice

サ	サ								
シ	シ								
ス	ス								
セ	セ								
ソ	ソ								

T Katakana Practice

タ	タ								
チ	チ								
ツ	ツ								
テ	テ								
ト	ト								

Character Memory Test

Try to identify the Hiragana character in the centre, which letter or sound does it represent?
Check your answer at the table on the introduction page.

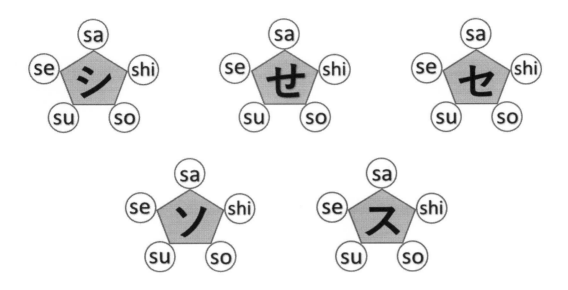

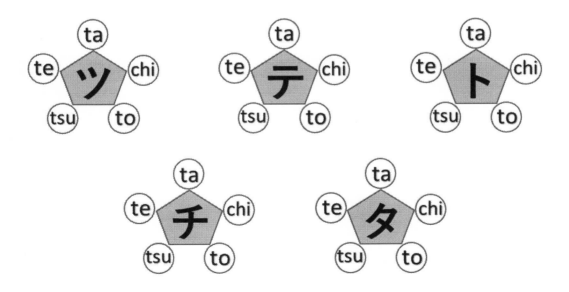

Sample Words Practice 2

If you have practiced the ten characters above you will already be able to write these words in Katakana:

Taxi (takushii) タクシー   Skiing (sukii) スキー   Curry & Rice (kareeraisu) カレーライス
Toast (toosuto) トースト   Coffee (koohii)　コーヒー

Practice these sample words below:

タクシー	タクシー		
スキー	スキー		
カレーライス	カレーライス		
トースト	トースト		
コーヒー	コーヒー		

N Katakana Practice

ナ	ナ								
ニ	ニ								
ヌ	ヌ								
ネ	ネ								
ノ	ノ								

H Katakana Practice

ハ	ハ								
ヒ	ヒ								
フ	フ								
ヘ	ヘ								
ホ	ホ								

Character Memory Test

Try to identify the Hiragana character in the centre, which letter or sound does it represent?
Check your answer at the table on the introduction page.

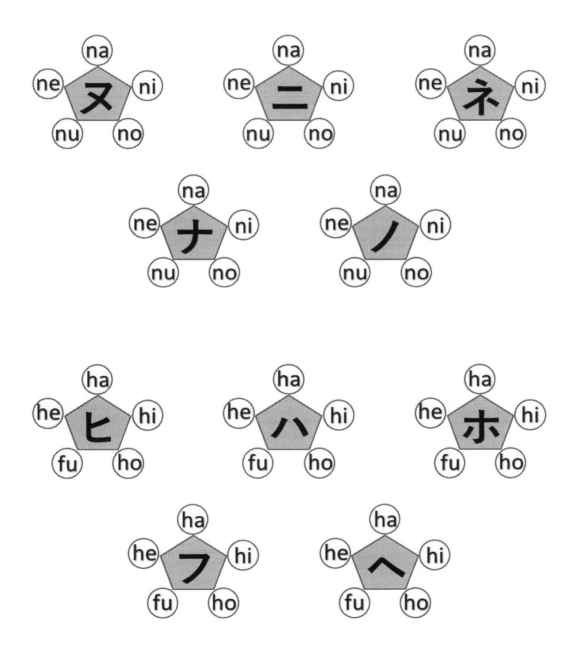

Sample Words Practice 3

If you have practiced the ten characters from N and H groups above you will already be able to write these words in Katakana:

Cola (koora) コーラ   Christmas (kurisumasu)クリスマス   Mobile Phone (keetai) ケータイ

Neck Tie(nekutai)ネクタイ   Fruit (furuutsu)   フルーツ

Practice these sample words below:

コーラ	コーラ		
クリスマス	クリスマス		
ケータイ	ケータイ		
ネクタイ	ネクタイ		
フルーツ	フルーツ		

M Katakana Practice

マ	マ									
ミ	ミ									
ム	ム									
メ	メ									
モ	モ									

Y Katakana Practice

ヤ	ヤ								
ユ	ユ								
ヨ	ヨ								

Y Katakana Practice

Character Memory Test

Try to identify the Hiragana character in the centre, which letter or sound does it represent?
Check your answer at the table on the introduction page.

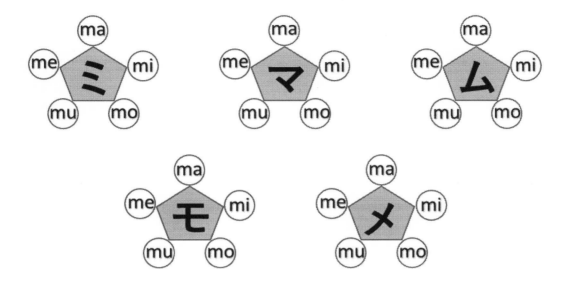

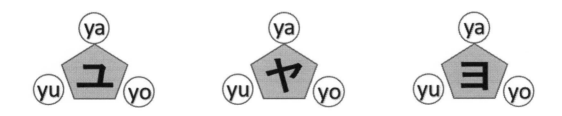

R Katakana Practice

ラ	ラ								
リ	リ								
ル	ル								
レ	レ								
ロ	ロ								

W and small n Katakana Practice

ワ	ワ								
ヲ	ヲ								
ン	ン								

Character Memory Test

Try to identify the Hiragana character in the centre, which letter or sound does it represent?
Check your answer at the table on the introduction page.

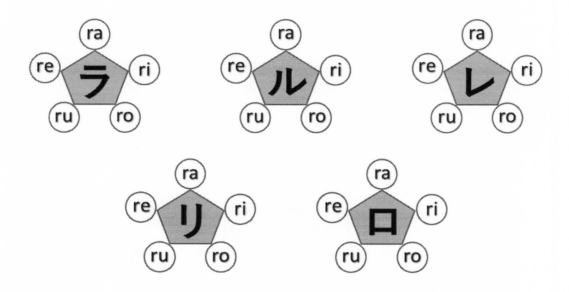

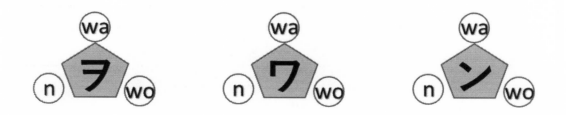

Sample Words Practice 4

If you have practiced all of the Katakana groups above you will already be able to write these words in Japanese:

Camera (kamera) カメラ   Cake (keeki)ケーキ   Anime (anime) アニメ

Restaurant (resutoran)レストラン   Skate (sukeeto) スケート

Practice these sample words below:

カメラ	カメラ		
ケーキ	ケーキ		
アニメ	アニメ		
レストラン	レストラン		
スケート	スケート		

Fill in the blank characters Test

Use your memory of the characters and your new handwriting skills to fill in the missing Katakana below.

	A	I	U	E	O
Vowels	__(A)	__(I)	ウ(U)	__(E)	__(O)
K	カ (Ka)	キ(Ki)	__(Ku)	__(Ke)	コ(Ko)
S	サ(Sa)	__(Shi)	ス (Su)	__(Se)	__(So)
T	__(Ta)	__(Chi)	__(Tsu)	テ(Te)	ト(To)
N	ナ (Na)	__(Ni)	__(Nu)	ネ (Ne)	__(No)
H	ハ (Ha)	__(Hi)	__(Fu)	__(He)	ホ (Ho)
M	__(Ma)	__(Mi)	__(Mu)	メ (Me)	モ(Mo)
Y	ヤ (Ya)		__(Yu)		__(Yo)
R	__(Ra)	リ (Ri)	ル(Ru)	__(Re)	__(Ro)
W	__(Wa)				ヲ (Wo)
N	__(N)				

Beginners Japanese – Katakana Stage Two

Modified basic Katakana Characters

	A	I	U	E	O
Vowels	ア (A)	イ (I)	ウ(U)	エ (E)	オ(O)
K	カ (Ka)	キ(Ki)	ク (Ku)	ケ (Ke)	コ(Ko)
S	サ(Sa)	シ (Shi)	ス (Su)	セ (Se)	ソ(So)
T	タ (Ta)	チ (Chi)	ツ (Tsu)	テ(Te)	ト(To)
N	ナ (Na)	ニ(Ni)	ヌ (Nu)	ネ (Ne)	ノ (No)
H	ハ (Ha)	ヒ (Hi)	フ (Fu)	ヘ (He)	ホ (Ho)
M	マ(Ma)	ミ (Mi)	ム (Mu)	メ (Me)	モ(Mo)
Y	ヤ (Ya)		ユ (Yu)		ヨ (Yo)
R	ラ(Ra)	リ (Ri)	ル(Ru)	れ (Re)	ロ(Ro)
W	ワ (Wa)				ヲ (Wo)
N	ン (N)				
G	ガ(Ga)	ギ(Gi)	グ(Gu)	ゲ(Ge)	ゴ(Go)
Z	ザ(Za)	ジ(Ji)	ズ (Zu)	ゼ (Ze)	ゾ(Zo)
D	ダ (Da)			デ(De)	ド(Do)
B	バ (Ba)	ビ(Bi)	ブ (Bu)	ベ(Be)	ボ(Bo)
P	パ (Pa)	ピ (Pi)	プ (Pu)	ペ (Pe)	ポ (Po)

The second group of Katakana characters are essentially modified versions of the first chart, shown here on the left.

Not every character from the first chart is modified. The full list is shown below.

The modifications change the sound of the character and are indicated above and to the right of the character as it is written.

You will notice the Ga ガ from Katakana appears below from the modified Ka カ character.

You will notice that " modifies the sound from Ka to Ga or from Te to De etc just the same as with Hiragana.

o Generally modifies a character to a P sound for example Ha becomes Pa, as shown below and within the P row adjacent.

Ka (カ) Ga (ガ)   Ha (ハ) Ba (バ) Pa (パ)

Hi (ヒ) Bi (ビ) Pi (ピ)   Te (テ) De (デ)

Writing Japanese Letters – G Katakana Practice.

Let's get back to practicing writing the letters that we will learn in order to write our first sentences in Katakana. Try to recreate each character in the boxes below. All Japanese characters will look slightly different in your own handwriting, get as close as you can to the printed versions.

While this may feel a little repetitive it will make your handwriting in Katakana start to take shape and help you remember the characters with repeated practice.

ガ	ガ								
ギ	ギ								
グ	グ								
ゲ	ゲ								
ゴ	ゴ								

Z Katakana Practice

ザ	ザ								
ジ	ジ								
ズ	ズ								
ゼ	ゼ								
ゾ	ゾ								

Character Memory Test

Try to identify the Hiragana character in the centre, which letter or sound does it represent? Check your answer at the table on the introduction page.

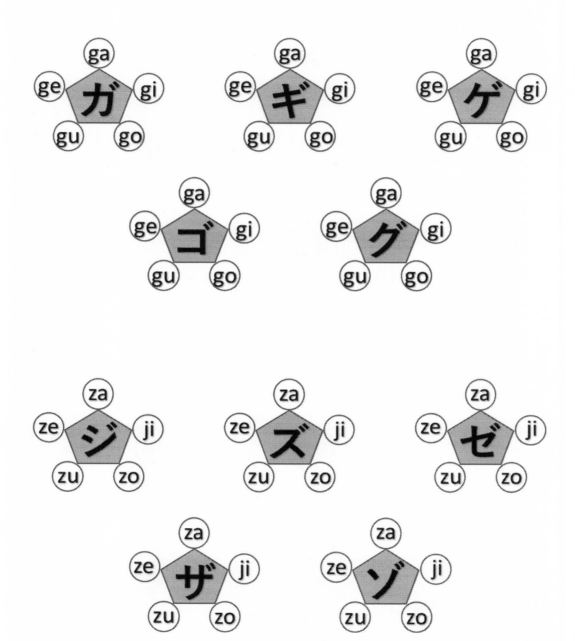

Sample Words Practice 1

If you have practiced the modified characters above, along with the previous lessons basic Katakana characters, you will be able to write these words in Japanese:

Asia (Ajia) アジア   Radio (Rajio) ラジオ   Piano (Piano) ピアノ   Cheese (ChiiZu) チーズ
Germany (Doitsu) ドイツ

Practice these sample words below:

アジア	アジア			
ラジオ	ラジオ			
ピアノ	ピアノ			
チーズ	チーズ			
ドイツ	ドイツ			

D Katakana Practice

ダ	ダ								
デ	デ								
ド	ド								

B Katakana Practice

バ	バ								
ビ	ビ								
ブ	ブ								
ベ	ベ								
バ	バ								

Sample Words Practice 2

Now try to write these words in Katakana:

Television (Terebi) テレビ Trousers (Zubon) ズボン Beer (Biiru) ビール
Party (Paateii)パーティー   Hamburger (Hanbaagaa) ハンバーガー

Practice these sample words below:

テレビ	テレビ		
ズボン	ズボン		
ビール	ビール		
パーティー	パーティー		
ハンバーガー	ハンバーガー		

P Katakana Practice

パ	パ									
ピ	ピ									
プ	プ									
ペ	ペ									
ポ	ポ									

Character Memory Test

Try to identify the Hiragana character in the centre, which letter or sound does it represent? Check your answer at the table on the introduction page.

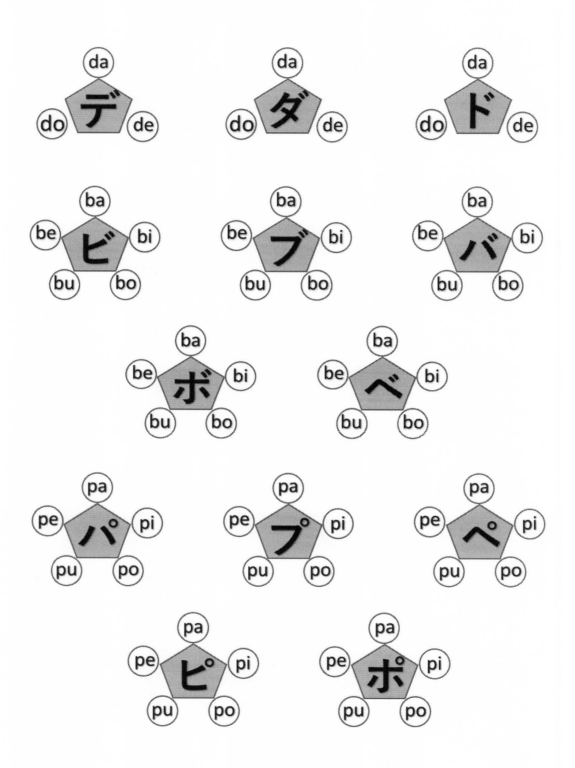

Sample Words Practice 3

If you have practiced the characters from the P group above you will already be able to write these words in Katakana.

England (Ingurando) イングランド   Whiskey (Waisukii) ウィスキー   Salad (Sarada) サラダ
Cappuccino (Kapuchiino) カプチーノ   Sandwich (Sando) サンド

Practice these sample words below:

イングランド	イングランド		
ウィスキー	ウィスキー		
サラダ	サラダ		
カプチーノ	カプチーノ		
サンド	サンド		

Sample Words Practice 4

If you have practiced all of the modified Hiragana groups above you will already be able to write these words:

Present (Purezento) プレゼント   Banana (Banana) バナナ   Bread (Pan) パン
Wine (Wiino)ワイン   Skirt (Sukaato) スカート

Practice these sample words below:

プレゼント	プレゼント		
バナナ	バナナ		
パン	パン		
ワイン	ワイン		
スカート	スカート		

Fill in the blank characters Test

Use your memory of the characters and your new handwriting skills to fill in the missing Katakana below.

G	__(Ga)	ギ(Gi)	__(Gu)	ゲ(Ge)	__(Go)
Z	ザ(Za)	__(Ji)	ズ (Zu)	__(Ze)	__(Zo)
D	ダ (Da)			__(De)	__(Do)
B	バ (Ba)	__(Bi)	__(Bu)	ベ(Be)	__(Bo)
P	__(Pa)	__(Pi)	__(Pu)	ペ (Pe)	ポ (Po)

Beginners Japanese – Katakana Stage Three

Modified Small Katakana Characters

The Katakana characters we have covered previously are shown below; new columns have been added to show the modifying characters. You will recognise them as a smaller version of the characters Ya, Yu and Yo from the Y row of Katakana characters:

	A	I	U	E	O	Ya	Yu	Yo
Vowels	ア (A)	イ (I)	ウ (U)	エ (E)	オ (O)			
K	カ (Ka)	キ (Ki)	ク (Ku)	ケ (Ke)	コ (Ko)	キャ (Kya)	キュ (Kyu)	キョ (Kyo)
S	サ (Sa)	シ (Shi)	ス (Su)	セ (Se)	ソ (So)	シャ (Sha)	シュ (Shu)	ショ (Sho)
T	タ (Ta)	チ (Chi)	ツ (Tsu)	テ (Te)	ト (To)	チャ (Cha)	チュ (Chu)	チョ (Cho)
N	ナ (Na)	ニ (Ni)	ヌ (Nu)	ネ (Ne)	ノ (No)	ニャ (Nya)	ニュ (Nyu)	ニョ (Nyo)
H	ハ (Ha)	ヒ (Hi)	フ (Fu)	ヘ (He)	ホ (Ho)	ヒャ (Hya)	ヒュ (Hyu)	ヒョ (Hyo)
M	マ (Ma)	ミ (Mi)	ム (Mu)	メ (Me)	モ (Mo)	ミャ (Mya)	ミウ (Myu)	ミョ (Myo)
Y	ヤ (Ya)		ユ (Yu)		ヨ (Yo)			
R	ラ (Ra)	リ (Ri)	ル (Ru)	れ (Re)	ロ (Ro)	リャ (Rya)	リュ (Ryu)	リョ (Ryo)
W	ワ (Wa)				ヲ (Wo)			
N	ン (N)							

You will notice that each column and each row have a title as these refer to the content of each syllable in the chart.

The second group of Katakana characters are essentially modified versions of the first chart. Not every character from the first chart is modified. The full list is shown below with the additional modifiers shown again in new columns.

G	ガ(Ga)	ギ(Gi)	グ(Gu)	ゲ(Ge)	ゴ(Go)	ギャ(Gya)	ギュ(Gyu)	ギョ(Gyo)
Z	ザ(Za)	ジ(Ji)	ズ(Zu)	ゼ(Ze)	ゾ(Zo)	ジャ(Ja)	ジュ(Ju)	ジョ(Jo)
D	ダ(Da)			デ(De)	ド(Do)			
B	バ(Ba)	ビ(Bi)	ブ(Bu)	ベ(Be)	ボ(Bo)	ビャ(Bya)	ビュ(Byu)	ビョ(Byo)
P	パ(Pa)	ピ(Pi)	プ(Pu)	ペ(Pe)	ポ(Po)	ピャ(Pya)	ピュ(Pyu)	ピョ(Pyo)

As before you will notice that " modifies the sound from Ka to Ga or from Te to De etc.

o Generally modifies a character to a P sound for example Ha becomes Pa, as shown below.

ツ A smaller version of Tsu is used to double the sound of the character that follows it and is seen often in Katakana. Placed before Ka for example (ツ カ) it becomes Kka when pronounced.

More Real-World Examples

The wording at the top of the sign says Kejan (ke-ja-n) in Katakana. It can be difficult to translate. This is why it is important to learn the characters well, so you can read that the crab is in a Cajun style sauce.

And one for coffee lovers. Can you decipher the names of the visible blends? Try re-writing the names character by character and maybe translating them into the English language version. They are quite small and will only sound like the English version. Give it a try.

Writing Japanese Letters – Modified K Katakana Practice.

Let's get back to practicing writing the letters that we will learn in order to write our first sentences containing Katakana. Try to recreate each character in the boxes below. All Japanese characters will look slightly different in your own handwriting, get as close as you can to the printed versions.

While this may feel a little repetitive it will make your handwriting in Katakana start to take shape and help you remember the characters with repeated practice.

Remember that the modifiers are just smaller versions of Ya, Yu and Yo that you learned in lesson 1 and these are always used after the character that they modify.

キャ	キャ					
キュ	キュ					
キョ	キョ					

Modified S Katakana Practice

シャ	シャ						
シュ	シュ						
ショ	ショ						

Modified T Katakana Practice

Although in the T group Chi is an exception as it begins with C of course. As with the others groups only one character is modified with Ya, Yu and Yo, in this case Chi ち is modified.

チャ	チャ						
チュ	チュ						
チョ	チョ						

Modified N Katakana Practice

This time only the character Ni ニ is modified with Ya, Yu and Yo.

ニャ	ニャ						
ニュ	ニュ						
ニオ	ニオ						

Character Memory Test

Try to identify the Hiragana character in the centre, which letter or sound does it represent?
Check your answer at the table on the introduction page.

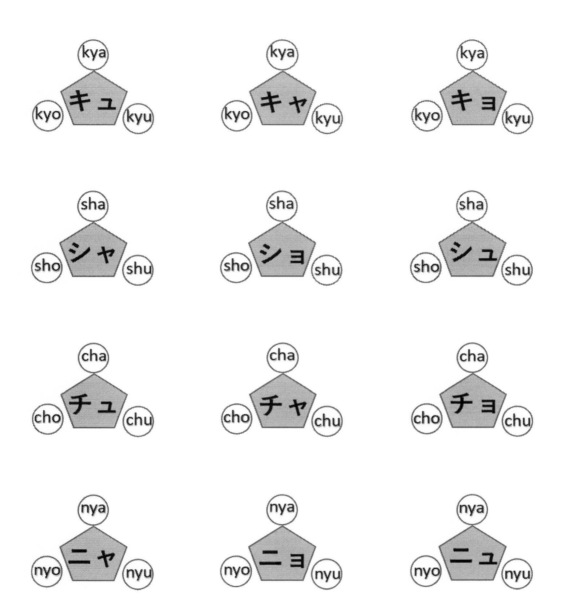

Modified H Katakana Practice

ヒャ	ヒャ						
ヒュ	ヒュ						
ヒョ	ヒョ						

Modified M Katakana Practice

ミヤ	ミヤ						
ミュ	ミュ						
ミヨ	ミヨ						

Modified R Katakana Practice

リャ	リャ						
リュ	リュ						
リョ	リョ						

Modified G Katakana Practice

ギャ	ギャ						
ギュ	ギュ						
ギョ	ギョ						

Character Memory Test

Try to identify the Hiragana character in the centre, which letter or sound does it represent?
Check your answer at the table on the introduction page.

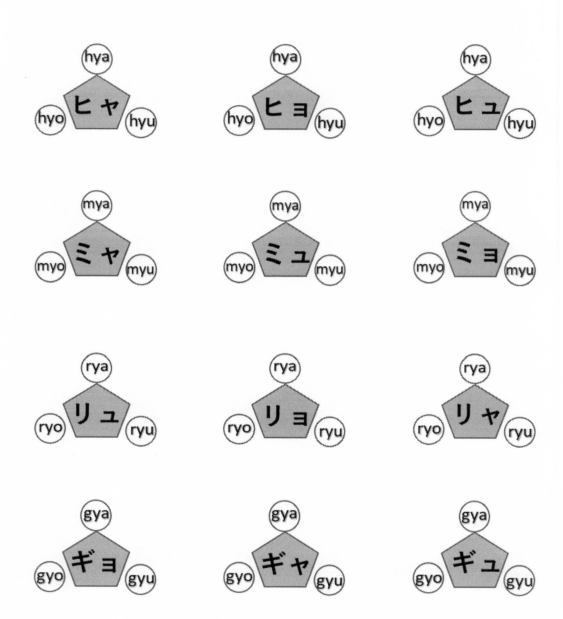

Modified Z Katakana Practice

Again, the Z character modified here is an exception in that it starts with Ji and not Z like Za, Zu Ze and Zo.

ジャ	ジャ						
ジュ	ジュ						
ジョ	ジョ						

Modified B Katakana Practice

ビャ	ビャ						
ビュ	ビュ						
ビョ	ビョ						

Modified P Katakana Practice

ピャ	ピャ						
ピュ	ピュ						
ピョ	ピョ						

Character Memory Test

Try to identify the Hiragana character in the centre, which letter or sound does it represent?
Check your answer at the table on the introduction page.

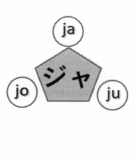 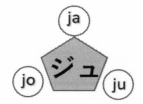 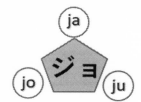

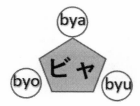 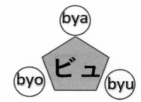 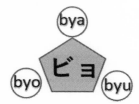

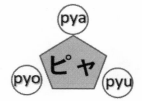 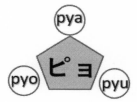 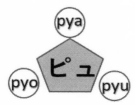

Writing Japanese Letters – Small Tsu ッ Meaning.

When the Katakana Tsu is used in the small form (the same as in Hiragana) it doubles the sound that follows it. Please note that it no longer has any use as Tsu when presented as the small form of Tsu, it only indicates that the sound of the character that follows it in a word is doubled.

Examples of real words are shown below.

Europe (Yuuroppa) ヨーロッパ   Espresso (Esupuresso) エスプレッソ
Lesson (Ressun) レッスン

ヨーロッパ	ヨーロッパ		
エスプレッソ	エスプレッソ		
レッスン	レッスン		

Sample Words Practice 1

If you have practiced the Ya (ヤ), Yu (ユ) and Yo (ヨ) characters you can write these words in Japanese:

Juice (Juusu) ジュース   Computer (Konpyuutaa) コンピューター   Shirt (Shatsu) シャツ
Hotdog (Hottodoggu) ホットドッグ   Shower (Shawaa) シャワー

Practice these sample words below, remember that the ヤ ユ ヨ should be written noticeably smaller than the other characters when using to modify their sound:

ジュース	ジュース		
コンピューター	コンピューター		
シャツ	シャツ		
ホットドッグ	ホットドッグ		
シャワー	シャワー		

Sample Words Practice 2

The bill (chekku) チェック   News (Nyuusu) ニュース   Gluten Free (Guruten Furii) グルテンフリー
Pizza (Piza) ピザ   France (Furansu) フランス

Practice these sample words below:

チェック	チェック		
ニュース	ニュース		
グルテンフリー	グルテンフリー		
ピザ	ピザ		
フランス	フランス		

Sample Words Practice 3

Menu (menyuu) メニュー　　Chocolate (Chokoreeto) チョコレート　　Guitar (Gitaa) ギター
Jumper/Sweater (Seetaa)セーター　　　　Lemon (Remon) レモン

Practice these sample words below:

メニュー	メニュー		
チョコレート	チョコレート		
ギター	ギター		
セーター	セーター		
レモン	レモン		

Fill in the blank characters Test

Use your memory of all of the characters and your new handwriting skills to fill in the missing Katakana below.

	A	I	U	E	O	Ya	Yu	Yo
Vowels	ア (A)	__(I)	__(U)	エ (E)	オ(O)			
K	カ (Ka)	__(Ki)	ク (Ku)	__(Ke)	__(Ko)	__(Kya)	__(Kyu)	キョ (Kyo)
S	__(Sa)	シ (Shi)	__ (Su)	セ (Se)	ソ (So)	シャ (Sha)	__(Shu)	__(Sho)
T	__(Ta)	__(Chi)	ツ (Tsu)	テ(Te)	__(To)	チャ (Cha)	__(Chu)	__(Cho)
N	ナ (Na)	__(Ni)	ヌ (Nu)	__(Ne)	__(No)	ニャ (Nya)	__(Nyu)	ニョ (Nyo)
H	ハ (Ha)	__(Hi)	フ (Fu)	__(He)	ホ (Ho)	__(Hya)	ヒュ (Hyu)	__(Hyo)
M	__(Ma)	__(Mi)	ム (Mu)	__(Me)	__(Mo)	__(Mya)	__(Myu)	ミョ (Myo)
Y	ヤ (Ya)		ユ (Yu)		__(Yo)			
R	ラ(Ra)	__(Ri)	__(Ru)	れ (Re)	__(Ro)	リャ (Rya)	__(Ryu)	リョ (Ryo)
W	__(Wa)				ヲ(Wo)			
N	ン (N)							

G	__(Ga)	__(Gi)	グ(Gu)	__(Ge)	ゴ(Go)	__(Gya)	ギュ (Gyu)	ギョ (Gyo)
Z	__(Za)	__(Ji)	ズ (Zu)	ゼ (Ze)	ゾ(Zo)	__(Ja)	__(Ju)	ジョ (Jo)
D	ダ (Da)			デ(De)	__(Do)			
B	__(Ba)	__(Bi)	ブ (Bu)	ベ(Be)	ボ(Bo)	ビャ (Bya)	__(Byu)	ビョ (Byo)
P	パ (Pa)	__(Pi)	プ (Pu)	__(Pe)	__(Po)	__(Pya)	__(Pyu)	ピョ (Pyo)

First published in Great Britain 2019

Beginners Japanese - Study Kana Hiragana & Katakana Learn to Read & Write in Japanese © 2019 by Danny Asser

Paperback edition published 2019

ISBN: 9781099026034

Asser, Danny (2019-02-05). Beginners Japanese - Learn Kana Hiragana & Katakana

Made in the USA
Middletown, DE
12 March 2020